ETHICS 101

Practical Ethical Guidelines
for Daily Living

OLAYINKA DADA, M.D.

authorHOUSE®

AuthorHouse™
1663 Liberty Drive
Bloomington, IN 47403
www.authorhouse.com
Phone: 833-262-8899

Published by AuthorHouse 01/13/2021

ISBN: 978-1-6655-0911-4 (sc)
ISBN: 978-1-6655-0910-7 (hc)
ISBN: 978-1-6655-0909-1 (e)

Library of Congress Control Number: 2020923677

Print information available on the last page.

Any people depicted in stock imagery provided by Getty Images are models, and such images are being used for illustrative purposes only. Certain stock imagery © Getty Images.

This book is printed on acid-free paper.

Contents

Acknowledgments ix

Chapter 1   Why Ethics? 1

Chapter 2   The Source of Ethics 3

Chapter 3   Cognitive Biases 9

Chapter 4   Character 19

Chapter 5   Conduct 35

Chapter 6   120 Ethical Pieces of Advice to Live By 39

Chapter 7   Financial Ethics (Honorarium) 57

Chapter 8   Ethical Areas to Watch 63

Chapter 9   Ethics, Excuses, and Misconceptions 79

Chapter 10 The Impact of Diminished Ethical

            Behavior 83

Epilogue   Real-Life Ethical Issues 87

To my spiritual parents—Pastor and Pastor (Mrs.) E. A. Adeboye—for showing and living the highest ethical standards for us to emulate.

Acknowledgments

First of all, I give God all the glory for the grace to finish this book. I am highly indebted to God's love, wisdom, favor, and blessings.

I also deeply appreciate my wife of more than twenty-five years for her love, loyalty, tolerance, and patience. I love you dearly.

My appreciation also goes to my spiritual parents— Daddy and Mommy Adeboye, the general overseers of the Redeemed Christian Church of God. I appreciate their love, impact, wisdom, and prayers.

I am also grateful to Mr. Ibukun Adeiye for his keen eyes and assistance in ensuring all the basic ethical areas are covered. I thank all members of Restoration House family for their loyalty, commitment, loyalty, and belief in the vision.

Lastly, I celebrate and appreciate our four children—Inioluwa Timothy, Oreoluwa Esther, Adeoluwa Mary-Favor, and Opeoluwa Deborah-Peace—for their understanding and willingness to uphold the ethical standards we teach at home. You are the best!

Chapter 1

Why Ethics?

A lot has changed in the twenty-first century. It seems as though the end is not in sight, as the level of moral decadence in the church and the world continues to rise. Interestingly, many Christians are not different from unbelievers in how they think. I have asked many questions about the reasons for the state of our land, and the answer I keep getting is that there is a lack of knowledge. Nobody seems to care about having a core foundation or a value system of any kind anymore. Good morals are not embraced and celebrated. Those who appear to stand for the truth are termed outdated.

Ethics are simply moral standards and guidelines we must know and follow. They are the truths we must walk toward or the gold standard we must achieve. Ethics define boundaries. Boundaries are necessary to ward off intruders and protect possessions.

Ethics also provide a guide for living. You cannot live your only life in a nonchalant manner. You need to know the dos and don'ts of life. Ethics help individuals avoid living a life of compromise and guide behaviors, especially in gray areas.

Ethics also hold you accountable. You are accountable to God, your spouse (if married), spiritual leaders, and one another. Without accountability, you can easily shipwreck your faith. You need people in your life who can help you grow, prevent you from falling into different sins, and lovingly tell you the truth when you error. You need someone who listens deeply to you, understands you, takes account of your entire story or past, and passes judgment that guides you to remain straight without a judging or critical spirit.

This book will focus on three key foundations of ethics: cognitive biases, character, and conduct. I also highlighted 120 ethical snippets of wisdom that I have found very helpful in my own Christian and leadership journeys. I hope you will find it useful and practical enough to implement.

Chapter 2

The Source of Ethics

In order to establish the source of ethics, we need to go to the very beginning. God is a God of order. It was a dark and chaotic world that prompted God to speak light, put everything intrinsically in place, and eventually introduce ethical guidelines to Adam and Eve.

Adam and Eve's relationships with God, animals, and other humans were clearly explained to them. The dignity of labor and hard work was inculcated into them by God. Invariably, God made it known to them that they were full of potential but had to unearth the numerous potentials through a life of discipline, industriousness, determination, sweat, and interdependence on others.

God also introduced the Ten Commandments to the Israelites as a way to guide their behaviors. The Bible is filled with ethical guidelines that should be the highest ethical standards by which we judge ourselves. The reasons are as follows:

- The Bible is God-inspired: "All scripture is given by inspiration of God and is profitable for doctrine, for reproof, for correction, for instruction in righteousness: That the man of God may be perfect, thoroughly furnished unto all good works" (2 Timothy 3:16–17 KJV).

- The Bible will not change: "The Words of God are constant. Heaven and earth will pass away, but My words will by no means pass away" (Matthew 24:35 NKJV).

- God honors His words: "For thou hast magnified thy word above all thy name" (Psalm 138:2 KJV).

- The Bible is infallible: "Sanctify them by Your truth. Your word is truth" (John 17:17 NKJV).

In the Bible, there are many examples on the rewards of obeying ethics as well as the repercussions of disobeying ethical guidelines. We are to learn from these examples to avoid repeating these mistakes:

Now all these things happened to them as examples, and they were written for our admonition, upon whom the ends of the ages have come (Corinthians 10:11 NKJV).

Today, nations have constitutions that dictate the fundamental rules and principles that govern a country. These are ethics by which a nation abides. Within these constitutions are the ethical standards expected of a country's citizens. Some of these national ethics may be contrary to the Word of God, but if any run afoul of it, they will be judged by it.

Unfortunately, some leaders of nations are not role models. As they flout the ethical guidelines of their nations, they are not held accountable or officially punished for the wrong they have done. This is the injustice of the present world, where the rich or the powerful have their way. This proves that no other ethical guidelines are as good as the one from the Creator of the universe. Moreover, the ethical standards of a nation keep changing from generation to generation, and they mainly depend on the views of the majority of those who can wiggle or manipulate the system.

Furthermore, organizations have policies, rules, and standards by which they operate. They tend to mainly emphasize integrity, professional competence, behavior, and confidentiality. These policies, rules, and standards are always put in place to ensure employees comply, and as a result, there is often a department that monitors the ethical behaviors of employees and enacts appropriate punishments for those who do not abide by these guidelines. Whether or not there is fairness in the way punishments are meted out for the violation of ethical standards is another thing.

Lastly, families or cultures have also set ethical guidelines to ensure their members comply. These may vary from one culture to another. They are also a function of prevailing religious beliefs, experiences, and traditions. These guidelines are also limited because the standards may be against the Word of God. For example, polygamy is celebrated by certain religions and cultures. In such a context, faithfulness to one spouse may not be a part of the ethical guidelines of such a family.

We cannot allow governments, organizations, cultures, or families to dictate our ethical standards because they change often and are as unstable as water. Most times, these ethical guidelines are born out of the views of the majority of those who speak the loudest.

In summary, the sources and standards of ethics we should live by should be:

- Global: not limited to countries, tribes, and tongues, and must apply to all human beings.

- Constant and applicable across civilizations and generations, not adjustable and amendable.

- Accessible: should be accessible by all.

- Not subject to different interpretations.

- Preeminent over cultures, science, innovations, and constitutions.

Chapter 3

Cognitive Biases

The dictionary defines bias as "a predictable tendency in thinking to favor one perspective over others." Biases blind our sight, blunt our judgments, blur our memories, and ultimately affect our decisions.

Environment, upbringing, exposure, and experiences play strong roles in our choices and decisions. These voices speak to us. The examples we emulate influence and tend to make us. Many people have adopted limitation thinking as a result of the type of family, city, and country from which they come.

Hundreds of biases have been highlighted through research. The following are just a few:

Blind Spot Bias

With this bias, you tend not to see your errors. We all make these errors, especially when we do not have people who tell us the truth. Very few people will tell you the truth. Many times, I have jumped up on my bed at night and realized the mistakes I have made in the past. I love having loved ones around me who can point out my errors. This is because in the thick of making decisions, we employ our most used or preferred processes with the inherent blind spot bias.

Affective Errors

There is an inclination to persuade yourself that what you want to be true is true instead of imagining less agreeable options. This is a common error when making decisions, especially when you use the yardstick of the world's definition of success. For example, there is a belief that doctors are rich and that many brilliant students are pushed into medicine by their parents even when they do not have an interest in it.

Ambiguity Bias

This is the tendency to make a choice with an outcome rather than an unfavorable one. While in Edmonton Canada, I once met a young man in the church protocol department who believed that any elevator must first come down before going up. Any time he was leading me to the elevator, he would first press the down button before pressing the up button. It reached a point where I had to ask him why he did this, and he explained his bias to me.

Ascertainment Bias

When your judgments are clouded by previous experiences, you are experiencing ascertainment bias. You find it difficult to be open to new experiences. I know a friend who was jilted many years ago. Today, she is still suspicious of people and finds it difficult to develop intimate relationships.

Bandwagon Bias

A tendency to follow the crowd can be called a bandwagon bias. We believe that the majority of rules carry us the right and best way. Many are following in the footsteps of popular opinions. With this bias, you do not take a stand based on convictions. God is not moved by the majority, but God does things according to His purposes.

Confirmation Bias

When you only reach for certain things or take a position regarding things that confirm your stand on the matter, you are exhibiting confirmation bias. Many people are so rigid to the extent that they are not open to new evidence or information. I have a friend who refuses to change from traditional paper files for patient records to electronic medical records. He is so passionate about paper filing, resistant to change, and can defend it to any extent without any form of apology.

Attribution Bias

When you always ascribe the cause of your problems or difficulties to a particular person or element and are not open to other possible causes, you are caught up in a bias of attribution. An example might be the belief that most illnesses are attributed to spiritual attacks or attacks from witches even when it appears your lifestyle or genes are playing a role.

Attentional Bias

The attentional bias is one in which you are affected by your recurring thoughts. This is common in people who commit one sin or another repeatedly. Many people from Africa tend to repeat "the blood of Jesus" during prayer when they hear it being mentioned.

Temporal Bias

Temporal bias is a bias where you feel guilty about what you have done in the past, and it is affecting your decisions today. You attribute any failures or negative happenings in your life to the sins you have committed in the past. Such people do not know or believe that your past is forgotten in the throne room of grace.

Implicit Bias

Implicit Bias is the unconscious association of particular traits or attributes to a member of a certain group, such as race. A personal experience I have with this topic stems from the hospital where I work in Ontario, Canada. Many patients have assumed that I am the cleaner, and others have even asked if I have treated a patient before allowing me to introduce myself as a physician.

These repeated encounters and experiences have caused me to produce answers to some of these funny questions by turning them into jokes. For example, when I am about to carry out minor procedures such as suturing of lacerations or reductions of joint dislocations, when asked if it is my first time performing it, I simply tell them it is and laugh it off. When I am asked where I am from, I say, "Ancaster, Ontario." If the person presses further and points out my accent, I tell them that is the way people speak in the area I live, and we laugh it off.

Other biases include the halo effect or authority bias, choice supportive bias, in-group preference bias, the ostrich effect, loss aversion or zero-risk bias, action bias, framing bias, and innovation bias.

Mitigating Against the Cognitive Bias

1. Increase your knowledge. Learn all the different cognitive biases, especially the ones that influence your decision-making process. Knowledge is power, and what you do not know can kill you. It

is important to seek knowledge. There is so much knowledge in the world today, many pieces of research have been done, and we are supposed to search these out. The knowledge of the truth will set us free. There is a story of a man who believes so much in witchcraft that he attributes anything that happens to him to witches from his father's house. He moved to Canada and started passing blood in his stool, but he thought the witches had followed him from Africa to Canada. He later shared his problem with a friend in the medical field. With information, counseling, and persuasion, he went for a colonoscopy, which revealed colonic polyps. The polyps were removed, and the rectal bleeding stopped. This man's experience transformed his mind.

2. Identify any cognitive distortions in your life. The purpose of knowing cognitive distortions is to be able to discover yourself. You need to investigate and examine in detail and apply what you have learned. This also involves being sincere with yourself. You never over-spiritualize your life to the extent that you gloss over your cognitive distortions, but you need to identify them. If you look carefully,

especially through the mirror of the Word of God, you will be able to see some patterns or distortions.

3.   Overcome all your prejudices. Get rid of all myths and prejudices. Be open to new ways of doing things. Be ready to unlearn and learn new things. Prayer is one of the ways we can overcome prejudices. You also need to be intentional to change. Know that there is nothing impossible; it just takes a little more time or a little more effort and faith. Our God can do all things. He knows no impossibility, and nothing is too hard for Him to do. If we believe God, we can overcome our prejudices.

4.   Grow in the Word of God. The truth sanctifies. "Sanctify them by your truth. Your word is truth" (John 17:17 NKJV). The Word of God is powerful and can clear all barriers out of your path. Let the Word of God dwell richly in your heart. Learn to speak the Word of God to your world. The Word will be a light that will consume every darkness of cognitive biases. Study to show you are approved unto God and rightly dividing the Word of truth. Be consistent and stay in the Word of God. Until you become intentional about growing, you will

never grow. You have to plan and be strategic about it.

5.   Confront your cultural biases. Challenge the status quo. Learn to probe further. Have a learning attitude and ask questions. Ask the right people the right questions at the right time and in the right way.

6.   Expose yourself to different options. Expand your thinking. Open your mind. Know that there are many ways to skin a cat or achieve something. Learn to evaluate your experiences. See what you can learn from your mistakes and challenge yourself from time to time. Never rest on your laurels.

7.   Use a trusted friend, buddy, or mentor as a check to help you in the process of identifying and providing you feedback in regard to your efforts to combat your biases. This friend acts as your active mirror, giving you unbiased feedback. This person needs to have a genuine interest in your success.

Chapter 4

Character

Character is who you are in private when no one is watching. Your character is developed in obscurity. What you are in the dark. What you do when no one is around you. This is who you are when accountability is not mandated or enforced by an authority figure or is completely nonexistent.

Character is also that thing about you that is constant and predictable. It is a constant effort to integrate your words, deeds, and actions:

> Daniel was a man of sound character as the Bible says no error or fault was found in him (Daniel 6:4 KJV).

Your words and actions must always match. Your character will be tested:

> For Joseph, his character was tested in the secret and quiet place in the house of Potiphar, his master. Potiphar's wife lured him and boldly said, "Lie with me" (Genesis 39:7 KJV).

For Job, after suffering one of the greatest losses of a lifetime—he lost his businesses and ten children—his wife prompted him to curse God:

> Dost thou still retain thine integrity? Curse God, and die. (Job 2:9 KJV)

Job retained his integrity, refused to curse God, and depended solely on God in the face of sufferings, afflictions, pressures, and pains.

A sound character will make you do what is right all the time. Whether a small or big thing, it does not matter. A person of sound character knows that small things also count as big things that are made up of small things. You do not cover up anything, but you can be depended on in any area of life.

A person of sound character is faithful, constant, loyal, stable, dependable, steadfast, and devoted. The person is faithful in his or her words, works, ways, friendships, appointments, and finances.

Like Paul, a person of character does not bow to pressure:

> We are troubled on every side, yet not
> distressed; we are perplexed, but not in despair;
> persecuted, but not forsaken; cast down, but
> not destroyed (2 Corinthians 4:8–9 KJV).

He or she does not behave like a tea bag that changes color and scent when dipped in hot water. Character is the foundation of any responsibility in life. No matter who you are, what privilege you have, or what position you occupy, if you don't have a sound character, you cannot not be relied upon. Your charisma may get you to any height or position, but it is your character that will sustain you there.

Gehazi was privileged to be the anointed assistant of Elisha. He witnessed many miracles firsthand. He even witnessed how General Naaman's leprosy was healed by swimming in the Jordan River, according to the instructions of Elisha. He lost his privileged position because of a defect in his character, and he coveted Naaman's wealth. Elisha, his boss, had refused to receive any gift from Naaman after healing him of leprosy, but Gehazi chased after Naaman to lie against his boss:

> So Gehazi followed after Naaman. And when Naaman saw him running after him, he lighted down from the chariot to meet him, and said, is all well?
>
> And he said all is well. My master hath sent me, saying, behold, even now there be come to me from mount Ephraim two young men of the sons of the prophets: give them, I pray thee, a talent of silver, and two changes of garments.
>
> And Naaman said, be content, take two talents. And he urged him, and bound two talents of silver in two bags, with two changes of garments, and laid them upon two of his servants; and they bare them before him.
>
> And when he came to the tower, he took them from their hand, and bestowed them in the house: and he let the men go, and they departed.

But he went in and stood before his master. And Elisha said unto him, whence comest thou, Gehazi? And he said, thy servant went nowhere

And he said unto him, went not mine heart with thee when the man turned again from his chariot to meet thee? Is it a time to receive money, and to receive garments, and oliveyards, and vineyards, and sheep, and oxen, and menservants, and maidservants?

The leprosy therefore of Naaman shall cleave unto thee, and thy seed forever. And he went out from his presence a leper as white as snow (2 Kings 5: 21–27 KJV).

Integrity

An important trait that enables us to be ethical in character is personal integrity. Integrity is the quality of being honest and having strong moral principles and moral uprightness. Before God, this is an admirable quality, and God boasted about Job's integrity.

An aspect of character wanes under pressure. A person of integrity will not succumb under pressure, but like Job, they will remain firm and resolute in doing what is right. To underscore the importance of integrity and loyalty, let us review the story of what happened to Job in detail.

Job and Integrity

Satan said to God, "And he will curse Thee to Thy face." The issue at stake here is loyalty of humankind to God. In all situations, humans will willingly choose to serve God, regardless of what we are passing through. Satan's position is that humanity simply seeks to use God, and God's position is that humans will willingly serve God not for benefit but by choice because it is the right thing to do. This is the integrity that God mentioned about Job (Job 1:9 KJV). Why am I serving God? Ethics requires self-accountability.

Why did God mention Job again? Was he the only righteous one on earth at that time? God said there is none like him on earth. He might not have been the only righteous man, but he was the best one.

Notice the condition God gave for being the best:

And the Lord said unto Satan, "Hast thou considered my servant Job, that there is none like him in the earth, a perfect and an upright man, one that fears God, and eschews evil? And still, he holds fast his integrity" (Job 1:8).

Integrity matters to God, He mentioned it in boasting about Job twice. Even Job's wife—prodded by Satan and the grief she had seen in Job—also mentioned it. It seemed to be the last straw or the final line of defense:

Do you still retain your integrity, curse God, and die (Job 2:9).

Integrity is the one thing the enemy cannot take from you because it is yours. It is integrity and not pride; both are very different. Pride emanates from something external like an achievement or a possession, but integrity comes from within and is based on innate beliefs.

Satan afflicted Job by moving from possession to personal pain to loss of life. This clearly shows that there is some form of hierarchy when it comes to what humans will prioritize or protect. Where will you place your integrity? Can yours be bought—or will you defend it with life itself?

Despite all the attacks, the Bible says Job did not sin with his lips. It is very easy—almost normal—for people to verbalize their frustrations or define issues with such clarity and show their anger, usually at God. However, Job's integrity will not allow him to take the easy option of complaining and blaming God for his misfortune.

Job did verbalize his frustrations, but from the point of view of nature, why was he born? If this would be his situation, why did he not die at childbirth? This was tending toward depression, but it was still not a grievance against God.

Job's friends tried their best to convince him of their logic—they did not have hindsight and went with the prevailing logic at that time—that he must have sinned and needed to repent before God for the "punishment" to stop. However, Job was equally insistent that he had done nothing wrong or deserved the treatment he was getting.

The three friends' position was that righteous people do not get punished. Their opinion was that only the sinners would go through Job's experiences—that God is infallible in His judgments—and they concluded that the only other explanation must be that Job had sinned and needed repentance. This was a direct attack, even an onslaught, on Job's integrity. He did not succumb to their strongly held positions because that would have been unethical. It would have been an admission of guilt when none existed.

Job felt hurt deeply by the words of his friends because they doubted his integrity and trampled on it with their logic and suggestions. We will face similar circumstances when we choose to stand for what is right. The integrity test here is passed when we choose not to compromise or lower our standards to please others.

For Job to be restored after the trying period, he needed to forgive and pray for his friends—in addition to asking for God's forgiveness—because they did not represent God accurately. Job needed to let go of the hurt and pain that they had caused him before he could move forward and possess what God had planned for him.

It takes grace to:

- know when we are being tested and even more grace to be able to hold onto our integrity—having the opportunity to cheat and refusing to.

- be calm, peaceful, and resolute in focusing on God.

- be able to maintain some level of civility and honor when we are being wrongly accused.

Like Job, it is quite possible that those closest to us can be used to challenge our integrity and test our faith in God, but we must hold fast.

Joseph and Integrity

We often face ethical dilemmas when we are in tight corners and feeling confused about what to do. Joseph was just seventeen years old when he faced such a dilemma. His blood brothers were actually considering killing him, but instead, they dumped him in a dry well and later sold him as a slave. However, his dilemma may well have started when he often brought back reports of his brother's dealings to their father. Was that the right thing to do?

Should we as Christians also report Christian brothers and sisters to the church leaders when we see them do wrong? Would that be the ethical thing to do? The right thing to do would be to advise the leadership, but there is a thin line that can be crossed here, especially with the intent and the mind-set when the reporting is done.

The goal should be to ensure that the brother or sister is quickly restored and not to make them the black sheep or to make them look appalling before the leaders. In Joseph's case, he decided to be loyal to his father and expose, even bring to light, the dark actions of his brothers. His brothers likely got scolded by their dad, and it made them dislike, even hate Joseph. Surely, and even at seventeen, he must have known this would happen!

When Joseph served in Potiphar's house, he faced even more challenging situations that would require him to draw endlessly on his store of integrity. His master's wife persisted in demanding he engage in an illicit and ungodly affair with her. On the one hand, he may have thought, if properly concealed, the proposed affair may bring him favors from the master's wife and ease his feeling of being let down by his brothers, but it would surely also mean his integrity would be wiped out completely. Worst of all, he would have sinned against God and possibly altered the course of his life and his destiny for life.

Joseph decided to retain his integrity before God, and he ran from a compromising situation. He chose to please God rather than humanity. Of course, there were consequences, and he ended up in prison. He was shamed for doing the right thing, but he retained his integrity.

Joseph faced several other dilemmas that are worth reviewing. He needed to tell it as he saw it when he was interpreting the dreams of the butler and the baker. There was no sugar coating to make the interpretations less gruesome, and he may have lied to gain human favor. He also needed to "attend to" his brothers when they came to Egypt to buy food for sustenance. Surely, this was a major test of character for him.

On the one hand, there was a human desire for revenge, retaliation, and humiliation of his brothers as due payback, and on another hand, he was seeing the bigger picture of what God wanted to achieve by sending him ahead into Egypt to preserve the lives of the children and descendants of Jacob.

These are difficult choices he needed to make and the kind that many of us face in our lifetimes. If I have the upper hand, will I seek revenge and punish those who offended me in the past by delaying my progress or even withholding what is clearly and rightfully mine? What is the ethical and Christian thing to do?

Joseph chose to forgive; he had lived thirteen years as a slave, either serving Potiphar or being in prison, yet he forgave as though the thirteen years of sorrow had never happened. He chose to retain his integrity rather than bring himself down to the level of his brothers. And since he forgave his brothers, he must have also forgiven Potiphar and his wife. This is evident because he was now at a higher position in society and he could have chosen to take his pound of flesh. After all, his word was now law and final in the land.

The story of Job and Joseph provide us with practical and real examples of ethical dilemmas that we also face from time to time today and for which we need to demonstrate our ethical standards through godly character and integrity to come out with flying colors.

Additionally, we can briefly mention Jephthah, who made an ill-advised vow by using the first thing that came out to welcome him from the battle, as a sacrifice. Unfortunately, it was his daughter who came out first, and being a man of integrity, he went ahead with the sacrifice.

We must realize that there are also examples of those who did not keep their word, and as such, they could not be regarded as men of integrity. Saul was a good example. He had stated openly to David and before his soldiers, after David spared his life, that he would no longer seek David's life. Alas, after just a little while, he was back on David's trail and trying to kill him. A person of integrity with good ethics will keep their word.

It is important to make clear that integrity is not prideful arrogance, and it does not have to be defiant. Joseph was firm but respectful in his refusal to compromise. Job refused to curse God. In our stance as men and women of integrity, we need not burn the bridges but rather provide a means by which the opposing forces could still come to realize their error and come to the light of what we hold so firmly.

It has also been said that someone can be sincere but sincerely wrong; how does this affect integrity? Well, before taking a stand on an issue, it is advisable to seek the truth and not just the "available facts" on that matter. Many are very quick to take a position based on limited information (and biases) and go to the extent of making judgments that will likely backfire and make such people have to eat their words.

A good example has been the source of the COVID-19 virus that was first identified in late 2019 and ravaged the world in 2020. Many staked their integrity on the fact that it all came from humans eating bats, and others swore that the virus was manufactured in a lab and somehow got out to start infecting humans. Even more surprising, some said it was caused by 5G telecommunications networks! It is possible that all three opinions could be wrong; however, reputable individuals have misled many of their followers— only to offer lame and poorly broadcasted rebuttals weeks later. Regardless, it is possible to mean well and still be wrong. After all, we are all striving for excellence and perfection. It takes a person of integrity apologize after realizing that their earlier position was erroneous. To avoid having to eat your words, it is wise to hold on and prove all things before taking a stand.

Being known as a man or woman of integrity buys us credits. In thorny situations, a person known for their integrity will be given the benefit of the doubt and will be believed. Building a solid reputation in the past seventeen years has enabled us to help the congregation entrusted to us. We have been able to contend for the release of some people who have experienced different kinds of issues with the law in our community because of our integrity and my professional status.

Joseph was found to be trustworthy and was always placed in positions of leadership in prison or Potiphar's house— at least when compared to other slaves and prisoners. A good indicator of whether you are viewed as a person of integrity and in excellent standing could be to determine what extent your words are believed or acted on by those in your close circle. Are they able to repeat what you have said as though it is the gospel truth—or would they prefer to check again or even disregard or ignore your statements entirely?

Chapter 5

Conduct

Conduct is the way you behave and act. It is your comportment and attitude. Conduct can be a function of education, background, culture, religion, exposure, personality, and choice.

Education can combat ignorance and impact our ability to follow guidelines and instructions, but some educated people still do not conduct themselves in the right ways. Being educated does not curb ignorance. Big words do not reflect knowledge.

Many people do not apply the knowledge they have. Some do not follow the right ethical guidelines. Some of the senior students in a predominantly White private school were found to exhibit racist behavior toward the few Black students despite the school promoting itself as an inclusive school to all. Some of the White students were misbehaving and intimidating their Black peers with questions such as "Can Blacks get tattoos?"

Culture is a way of doing things in a particular place and among a particular group of people. Culture can determine the perception of threats. For example, the panic-buying of tissue paper during the outbreak of the coronavirus was popular in developed nations like North America, but in Africa and the Middle East, alternatives to tissue paper were promoted in the culture. Also, the outbreak of coronavirus has led to the wearing of facial masks, which is seen as a strange thing in North America, is an integral part of some cultures.

Religion also plays a great role in our conduct. For some people, dressing is based on their interpretation of the scriptures. We also see some people who do not care about covering their cleavage because they believe their religion permits it. It is also disheartening that some people's interpretations of the scriptures have led to the worst conduct in human history, including murder, rape, and maltreatment of Black folks during apartheid of South Africa.

Exposure in terms of experiences and travels to other cultures and places can affect conduct. In some African countries, corruption is part and parcel of their way of life. This is not condoned in many developed nations.

I have had colleagues who traveled from North America to Africa and subsequently left in anger because of the level of frivolousness, lack of respect for time, and corruption in the country. What also surprised my professional colleagues is the way these negative conducts are ingrained in the fabric of the populace of the entire nation. People have come to accept it as a way of life. Furthermore, because of the underexposure of some of our African uniformed men, the level of their brutality is unimaginable. They still severely maltreat those they should be protecting.

One's personality can also determine their behavior. Some people overreact to situations and behave extremely, and others underreact or behave in other unacceptable manners.

Paul commanded the Philippian Christians and taught his protégé, Timothy, how to conduct himself:

> Those things, which ye have both learned, and received, and heard, and seen in me, do: and the God of peace shall be with you (Philippians 4:9 KJV).

> I write so that you may know how you ought to conduct yourself in the house of God, which is the church of the living God, the pillar and ground of the truth (1 Timothy 3:15 NKJV).

There are codes of conduct for employees, employers, church members, parents, children, and Christians:

> Let no man despise thy youth: but be thou an example of the believers, in word, in conversation, in charity, in spirit, in faith, in purity (1 Timothy 4:12 KJV).

Paul told Timothy that he should be a model in his conduct:

- Be holy or godly.

- Be a servant.

- Be courteous.

- Be grateful.

- Be humble.

- Be diligent.

Chapter 6

120 Ethical Pieces of Advice to Live By

Relationships

1.   Your word must be your bond. Integrity must be your watchword. Even when it results in temporary hurt or loss, the long-term effect is positive and beneficial.

2.   Have boundaries. Boundaries give people space. Even your children need their space. Avoid barging in on people no matter your excuse.

3.   Honor all people. I know those who truly honor me by the way they honor my spouse.

4. Make provision in your daily routines to touch one life daily. You may need to lend your ears to someone who needs a person to talk to. Make it a point to add value to others with every interaction; even making a sad person see the brighter side of life with a smile is adding value.

5. Be flexible and learn to adapt to other cultures. When you get to a new environment, study and understand the culture and then flow with it, provided it is not against the will or Word of God. This gives you a head start at settling down and reaching the people in that area.

6. Be patient. There is a virtue in patience. Be patient with your unreasonable partner, child, employee, employer, or boss. You will win the war with your patience.

7. Be kind to others. Do not forget that whatever you sow, you will reap.

8. Show respect. Treat elders with dignity. Don't provoke, ignore, or despise the younger ones.

9. Celebrate with people.

10. Avoid unnecessary closeness with the opposite sex other than your spouse.

11. Get along with others. Be at peace with other people.

12. Be kind. Learn to treat others with respect, have engaging and challenging conversations, and learn the art of listening (Ephesians 4:32 KJV).

13. Let your stance on issues and your belief and faith be well-known.

Personal Ethics

14. Control your emotions and never lose your calm in arguments and discussions. Learn to hear other opinions and learn the art of listening. This will take time and painstaking effort.

15. Do not be hasty. Wait for your season. To everything, there is a season and a time to every purpose under the heaven. Results come from God—just be faithful and do your part excellently.

16. Have accountable partners. People will be given the right to evaluate your actions and speak the truth

to you. They give you 360-degree views of your actions. They help you remain true to yourself, in the faith, and abide by the narrow and long road of life.

17. Be open to change. Do not close up on people or situations around you. Accept all, irrespective of their choices or colors or behaviors as God's masterpiece. In this world, people come in different shapes, sizes, colors, behaviors, and orientations.

18. Be of a sound character. Do not let yourself be judged by anything other than your character and faith.

19. Learn the power of forgiveness. Do not keep scores of wrongs. Unforgiveness is like dirt in a pipe; it makes you stink and clogs you up, leading to all kinds of stresses and diseases.

20. Take responsibility for your actions. The easiest thing in life is to make excuses and play the blame game. Owning up to your errors is a pathway to growth and restoration. After the fall of humankind in the Garden of Eden, Adam blamed Eve for his actions, Eve blamed the devil, and the devil blamed

God. Passing the buck like this creates complications as illustrated when they were punished for their actions by God.

21. You should carry yourself well. Do not lose your confidence or self-esteem. No matter your past or status, you have the DNA of God.

22. Be humble. Avoid exaggerated self-esteem. Avoid taking the glory. Avoid putting attention on yourself.

23. Dress well (not necessarily expensively). Be modest in your dressing and be comfortable in what you wear. Avoid exposing sacred parts of your body that are meant for your spouse alone. Because the world is enhancing its femininity or masculinity through flirting or seduction does not make it right for a child of God.

24. Work on your self-control. Be disciplined enough to master your senses and grow to a level to control your spending, sleeping, eating, drinking, and sexual impulses.

25. Watch your words. Avoid negative words and rants. Do not speak F-words and avoid unholy jokes. Be authentic with your words. There is no need to lie. People already know that no human is perfect, and we all have what we struggle with in this world of sin. They will relate better to you if they know you also have failures and frailties.

26. Have a good name. A good name is better than gold and silver. Do not be known as a quarrelsome or cantankerous person.

27. Acknowledge all gifts.

28. Return all calls, emails, or messages within twenty-four hours if possible.

29. Show gratitude. Don't forget kind deeds. Make a habit of expressing gratitude.

30. Exercise daily. It is profitable, and about 150 minutes a week is recommended.

31. Rest well. It is a good way of refreshing your soul, mind, and body. Observe the Sabbath (Exodus 20:8 KJV). Appreciate nature. Listen to the birds' songs.

Smell the flowers. Calm down, meditate, and hear your heartbeat.

32. Do not mask your emotions. It is recorded that Jesus wept openly by the grave of Lazarus, his friend.

33. Do not be in a hurry or hasty.

34. Put your trust in God by praying daily.

35. Do not retaliate (Proverbs 24:29 KJV). "Vengeance is mine," says the Lord (Romans 12:19 KJV)

36. Be on the lookout for and maximize opportunities, including volunteering, to add value and devote part of your time to help humankind. It's part of contributing value and making your life count.

37. Laugh more. It's medicine for the soul.

38. Do not lose your identity or interests.

39. Be dedicated to improving yourself. Do not be satisfied with mediocrity.

40. Trust God completely (Proverbs 3:5 KJV). God is to be trusted. Rest in God even in difficult and

tough times. Tough times do not last—but tough people do. Let God fight your battles and wars.

41. Study to be quiet. Silence is golden, and it cannot be misquoted (Proverbs 17:27 KJV). A fool is considered wise if he keeps quiet (Proverbs 17:28 KJV).

42. Be holy and righteous (1 Thessalonians 5:22 KJV). God will not change His standards for you. There are no shortcuts. The longest distance between two posts is the shortcut.

43. Rejoice always (1 Thessalonians. 5:16 KJV). Laughter is good medicine.

44. Do not be obsessed with yourself. Do not get carried away with your accomplishments.

45. Take some risks. Not taking risks is risky. Leave your comfort zone—and keep stretching.

46. Learn to ask questions.

47. Give your heart to wisdom. Wisdom gives life. It preserves life.

48. Do not be lazy (Proverbs 24:30–34 KJV).

49. Be a good citizen, abide by the laws, and honor those in governmental authority.

50. Avoid jokes with lies, jesting, and pranks.

51. Be a great giver (Acts 20:35 KJV; Luke 6:38 KJV). Change the world's erroneous belief that there is no free lunch. Always look for what you can give rather than what you can take or benefit.

52. Avoid borrowing (Proverbs 22:7 KJV).

53. Do not be surety for a stranger.

54. Be prudent, avoid unnecessary expenses, and develop your financial acumen so you can be a giver to worthy causes.

55. Do not live above your means. It will come back to hurt you, and the people you seek to impress will end up mocking you.

At Work or in an Organization

56. Be hardworking. Hard work pays. Learn to be diligent.

57. Be on time. Avoid lateness, value other people's time, and be the exception who is always on time.

58. Resignation must not be a surprise move. Learn to give notice of resignation. I recommend three to six months of written notice before resignation. At a minimum, follow the resignation guidelines of your organization.

59. Do not disagree openly with your leader. No leader is perfect. Try to avoid arguments and faultfinding.

60. Do not be disloyal. The test of a good leader is found in being a good follower.

61. Find a leader and serve them. Honor your leaders. Esteem them (1 Thessalonians 5:12–13 KJV). Learn how to genuinely admire and praise your leader.

62. Be intentional.

63. Do not find faults.

64. Do not disrespect them.

65. Be professional with your communication. Be classy and not creepy.

66. Respect people's time. Do not be a busybody.

67. Learn the art of preparation (Proverbs 21:31 KJV).

68. Watch your associations (Proverbs 22:24 KJV).

69. Do not try to undercut or undermine others to make yourself look good. Absalom's example is a case in point.

70. Always be willing to help where you can—and you will get help when you need it.

71. Do unto others as you would like them to do to you.

72. Provide positive criticisms privately but commend publicly.

73. Be aware of the goals of your organization and be guided by them.

As a Leader or a Parent

74. Be a learner. Seek knowledge. Read books. Learn, unlearn, and relearn.

75. Do not condemn.

76. Do not be drunk with power. Power corrupts and can cloud judgment (Hosea 4:6 KJV).

77. Travel wide, expose yourself, and be open to fresh ideas.

78. Do not judge.

79. Keep your head on straight, listen more, and speak less.

80. Never stoop to the level of naysayers, backbiters, or critics.

81. Do not fight all battles; otherwise, you will be weary.

82. Value hard work.

83. Keep confidential information.

84. When you make mistakes, admit them quickly— and try to learn from them.

85. Do not be a phony. Do not put on an act.

86. Learn to be vulnerable.

87. Put people first. Service is all about people (Galatians 6: 10 KJV).

88. Add value to others (Galatians 6:7 KJV).

89. Be authentic. Share your personal stories, especially your struggles. People relate well to personal stories and experiences.

90. When you hire, hire those who have hearts of service rather than mercenaries (Hebrews 11:6 KJV). Teach the reward of service.

91. Provoke greatness in people. Help them discover their potential.

92. Demand nothing less than loyalty from your core leaders. It starts with orientation and constant training (Luke 16: 12–13 KJV). Loyalty is rare to find; when you find one who is loyal, celebrate the person.

93. Have core values and communicate them all the time.

94. Learn to clearly share your vision while taking responsibility and celebrate milestones when

you attain them (Habakkuk 1:1–3 KJV). Always articulate your vision. Say it in ways that resonate with people.

95. Think about your legacy. What impact are you building? David served and impacted his generation (Acts 13:36 KJV). What are people learning from you? Teach the value of a strong work ethic, humility, honesty, and mutual respect.

96. Be purposeful and focused (1 Corinthians 9:25–27 KJV).

97. Create a loving environment (1 Thessalonians 3:12 KJV).

98. Create an environment where no one is judged and an environment that makes people feel encouraged and comfortable to take risks and share ideas.

99. Welcome new ideas and thoughts. No one should make fun of anybody.

100. Introduce "Got an idea?" Show no bias against gender, race, cultural background, spiritual level, or age.

101. Always foster and assume the best intentions of others.

102. Give back to your community (1 Thessalonians 5:14 KJV).

103. Have a winning mentality. Always be positive.

104. Be closer to your people. Be there to celebrate their important milestones.

105. Never neglect your family (Hebrews 2:3 KJV). If we neglect family, how shall we escape dysfunctional posterity?

106. Attempt change. Paul said, "I die daily" (1 Corinthians 15:31 KJV). Apply the principle of 1 percent gains. A one percent change may not sound like much, but small improvements in the way you live each day and every day will amplify your life. It can turn good to great. Being better by just one percent every day is like compound interest for your body, mind, family, and organization.

107. Forgive easily. Avoid bitterness. Never allow the root of bitterness in your heart. It defiles, and

the roots of bitterness take time to be rooted out (Hebrews 12:15 KJV; Mark 11:25 KJV).

108. Train up your children and those around you (Proverbs 22:6 KJV).

109. Learn to humble yourself and seek counsel (Proverbs 24:6 KJV).

110. Pray always (1 Thessalonians 5:17 KJV).

111. Do not be partial.

112. Don't put trust in humans (Proverbs 25:19 KJV).

113. Do not reward evil for good.

114. Be thankful (1 Thessalonians 5:18 KJV). Avoid complaining. It complicates matters.

115. Watch your words.

116. Have a plan with checkpoints to measure your progress—and take appropriate actions based on the extent of your progress to achieve that plan.

117. Be an encourager, especially of those who are timid but have great ideas. Encourage participation and inclusivity.

118. Recognize people's contributions and commend them.

119. Manage down biases by encouraging a diversity of ideas.

120. Try to avoid second-guessing others and be open instead of shady and manipulative.

Chapter 7

Financial Ethics (Honorarium)

Many have compromised their faith because of their reckless financial spending. Money should always be seen as a tool in our hands rather than an instrument to derail us.

I want to highlight an aspect of financial ethics in this chapter, and that is about *honorariums*. An honorarium is a payment given for professional services provided in which a price is not set. The host decides how much is given for the services rendered, and as a result, it leaves room for abuse or ill feelings. I am of the opinion that it should always be substantial. Do not turn honorarium to "dis-honorarium!" It should be given from a heart of love, generosity, and honor.

Ignorance of how honorarium is given is a common thing because it is not taught. I was invited by a friend to be the guest speaker at their annual conference. Their church had been in existence for about seven years. The anointing was very heavy, and many were touched and rose up to the challenge of supporting the church's new project.

After my session, I was given a very small honorarium that would hardly cover my travel expenses. In my characteristic manner, I appreciated the gift. The same pastor invited me three years later, and out of my busy schedule, I went. At the end of the conference, he gave me the same honorarium as three years prior. It dawned on me that maybe the pastor had not been taught the ethics of honorarium. I know many of his conference speakers will not be speaking for him more than once if he does not learn the art of honoring them well.

I prayed about it and came up with a game plan for enlightening him on the subject matter provided he allowed me to return the gift. We both agreed when he saw my heart that I was coming from a place of informing and not exploiting or receiving. During our session together, I was excited to know it was done out of ignorance because no one had ever taught him how to honor guest ministers, and he was open to learn. I also learned a great lesson that you cannot expect what is not taught. I have taken it upon myself to inform those around me about the proper honorarium guidelines.

As a physician, I have received honorarium for lectures, especially from pharmaceutical companies, and I discovered through many years of interactions that they have guidelines too. The amount is based partly on your specialty, years of experience, expertise, and conference attendance.

Paul the apostle also instructed his protégé, Timothy, about how to honor ministers of the Gospel:

> The elders who direct the affairs of the church well are worthy of double honor, especially those whose work is preaching and teaching. For Scripture says, "Do not muzzle an ox while it is treading out the grain," and "The worker deserves his wages" (1 Timothy 5:17–18).

Paul highlights in this passage that we should give ministers of the Gospel twice as much honor as we would give to other professionals or leaders. Double honor also applies to doubling their honorarium in reference to other professionals and leaders!

In processing a good honorarium for guest speakers, the following guidelines have helped me a great deal in our ministry. These are the questions we often ask ourselves before deciding the amount:

1. Are they a general overseer? In other words, are they the founder or most senior pastor of the church? Do they have many churches under them?

2. What is their leadership position in the ministry/ mission? For example, in the Redeemed Christian Church of God, we have the following organogram (in descending order): assistant general overseer, special assistant to the general overseer, regional pastor, provincial pastor, zonal coordinator, area pastor, parish pastor, ordained minister, head of department, and worker.

3. Is the person an expert in a field? For example, on the subject of leadership, John Maxwell or Sam Chand are generally regarded as experts.

4. What is the number of speaking engagements? This is the number of times (nights/days) you have asked them to speak in your church.

5. What are the sacrifices the guest is making? Is the speaker sacrificing their Sunday in their home church to attend and speak in your church or program?

6. Did you invite the speaker specifically for your program—or were they visiting of their own accord (a "walk-in") and you asked them to speak? Are you bringing them from their base—or are they passing through your city for another entirely different engagement and you are just trying to take advantage or honor the person by giving up your pulpit for that particular day?

7. How much are we spending on their transportation and accommodation?

8. What is the size of the guest speaker's church, especially if they are sacrificing their Sunday?

9. What is the impact or long-term value the guest minister is bringing to your assembly? This is determined by the way the speaker or rally draws people (attendance), culminating in the growth of your ministry, spiritual impartation in terms of testimonies and other gains such as open doors, future relationships, and financial rewards.

Just as it is unethical for any guest speaker to make a financial demand from the host, it is also unethical to bring a guest without honoring them very well. Remember that what is worth doing is worth doing well, and we often do not get a second chance to correct a first impression.

However, there are times the host church or organization may not have the financial muscle to host a desired guest minister, especially those who are high up in the hierarchy of the church or organization. Instead of digging oneself into a financial hole, it is advisable to discuss this beforehand with the guest speaker or their contacts to manage their expectations. I have returned honorariums a few times to alleviate the financial burdens my time will place on my host church. I am of the opinion that any guest speaker invited should be a blessing in every way rather than a burden.

An honorarium is not the only way to appreciate or honor your guest ministers. There is also the need to have excellent protocol and hospitality teams, a neat environment, royal services, and such in place to give them a unique experience and wonderful memories of their time with you.

Chapter 8

Ethical Areas to Watch

Conflicts of Interest

Nepotism

This is the act of favoring relatives and/or friends in what should normally be competed for; this includes contracts and jobs. This includes preferential treatment and unfair treatment. In many cultures, practices like this are tolerated or even encouraged, which only serves to deny the best candidates the opportunities they deserve.

In certain societies, this practice is justified by statements like "Everyone does it" or "It's an accepted practice." Good ethical behavior requires us to do the right thing—all the time. We must note that this is different from networking, which is about relating to people in different or similar fields of interest for the purpose of sharing knowledge. Regardless of the pressures from society, we have to be accountable to God and hold ourselves accountable to ensure that we do the right thing instead of excusing it away. We cannot be outstanding if we behave like the people of the world and do what every other person does. We must allow our light to shine very brightly so that others will notice the difference and be attracted to the light.

Abuse of Power or Authority for Personal Gain

This is becoming a cultural issue in many countries. The concept and advent of macho men in power as something that some admire is even more relevant today, especially on the global political front. However, the well-known statement about absolute power corrupting absolutely applies to various levels and not only those leading nations. Even a gateman can abuse his power by preventing access to legitimate items, demanding bribes, or allowing items and persons who do not meet entry guidelines simply because such people bring him personal gains at the detriment of an immense risk to the organization.

So, pretty much everyone has the potential to abuse whatever power (however small) they have. It is similar to parents abusing their kids physically and emotionally simply because they can. The true worth of a leader is measured in the ability to be restrained and measured in the exercise of such powers and ensuring that the exercise of such powers is fully in line with the reason for being vested with such powers in the first instance. That would be the ethical thing to do.

The application of appropriate discretion and counsel in the exercise of powers would significantly aid the retention of ethical delivery in any role. We must recognize that it is quite easy to overstep our boundaries and continue to do so if one has been doing so for long. With time, it gets normalized—and that is very dangerous. It is better to exercise caution and separate personal concerns and issues from the organization one belongs to.

I Scratch Your Back and You Scratch Mine

This is a form of collusion between two or more people to do wrong. This compromises the integrity and personal ethics of those involved—usually at the expense of any organization or country that such people belong to. Several under the table business transactions are likely executed in this manner. Some monopolies and cartels are formed based on this, basically to protect each other's interests at the expense of others.

The act of giving and receiving bribes also falls into this category, including all the shady ways in which bribes are given either as a gratuity before or after an event. These gratuities are sometimes given to relatives of the principal to avoid traceability by financial institutions. Let us be careful to ensure that the motive behind our actions—genuine and appropriate appreciation for a good deed done—are in order. Even a simple thank you might suffice. However, once actions are taken for the purpose of reciprocity, we need to check such motives to ensure they are ethical.

Compromising Scenarios

Familiarity Breeding Sin

One can argue that the incident between Joseph and Potiphar's wife could have been stoked by familiarity between them. Familiarity leads to a letting down of one's guard, which can lead to compromising situations, especially between members of the opposite sex. This is similar to the process of planting spies within an organization. A spy can become so well-known and trusted over time that they are granted access to secrets that can be used against the organization.

Christians in courtship—yet to be legally married—are often admonished not to be together alone in locations where no one else can see them because emotions can be aroused, which can lead to them defiling themselves. Many taunt their self-control and ability to resist such temptations, but the best recommendation in situations like that is to flee all appearances of evil. We are not to rely on human knowledge or inner strength to fight this one; the recommendation is to run.

Samson stayed with the harlot, and his destiny was tragically altered. Joseph chose to run and safeguarded his destiny. We are encouraged to take heed when we think we are standing: I will not drop my guard, I will identify the danger, and I will take immediate action to amend and not assume I am strong enough to deal with it when the issue is no longer manageable.

Pressured into Shady Actions

Our everyday interactions with people force us to shape or be shaped by goings-on around us that have been dictated by others. The extent of our noncompliance with the opinions of others around us dictates the amount of pressure we are subjected to make us bend and not remain outliers. Now, if it so happens that the few around us or a large proportion of the populace are breaking the law—for example, choosing to drive into oncoming traffic or believing that public office is primarily meant for personal business advantage or the enrichment of allies and patrons—to what extent do we bow to such pressures based on such being the norm? Ethical behavior requires us to be fully persuaded, be unflinching in our positions, and be proponents of ethical positions regardless of being outliers.

We are to interact and influence others and provide counterpressure to the norm. For most of us, these pressures start with peer pressure from our small four- or five-person cliques and run to high-level lobbying groups with deep pockets. There are pressures from every side, and our firm resolve on what is ethically right and the courage to pursue the same will be key. Publicly and frequently declaring our ethical resolve can help us manage and deflate these pressures.

Jesus also faced these types of pressures, but He chose to be public with His position. He engaged many people, including the leaders of the day, and He used the Word of God as His basis. The entire populace could identify with challenging the status quo and trying to change erroneous and long-held perceptions. Being fully persuaded Himself, He spoke with authority as someone who knew what He was talking about. He spoke loudly and to large crowds, influencing many to rethink their positions. He painted a picture of what the norm should be—the standard is the kingdom of God—and He enabled the people to see the extent of departure from that standard. Thus, He demonstrated how to be able to articulate the first and simple steps that must be taken to restore normalcy.

In summary, we must know what is ethically right, stand firm on this, and go on to influence others to adopt the same standard. Otherwise, we will be swept off with every wind of doctrine, and we will bend to every pressure we are subjected to.

Personal Ethics Scenarios

White Lies and Exaggerations

Our ethical standards are daily measured in the way we communicate with others, argue our positions, and seek to bring others on board with our views. Some believe that little embellishments here and there are not so bad as long as the end objective is met, but this way of thinking is wrong. Unfortunately, the end does not justify the means; the process also matters. It is quite possible to communicate cleanly and ethically and even win arguments when we have done our homework properly. It is important not to feel pressured into having to lie or embellish, and to achieve this, preparation and composure are the two key items we need.

As part of the preparation, we must establish firm foundations and boundaries that we will not compromise in any situation. These boundaries will help put us in check when we could otherwise have gone astray. An example of a boundary is how long we talk (the duration). Once we reach the planned duration, we excuse ourselves and keep quiet. Another boundary could be when we start feeling the pressure to speak over others. At that point, we refrain and keep quiet because that pressure is often a precursor to exaggerations. Each of us needs to note what the precursors are for us and establish those as boundaries.

Another important boundary to consider is the quality of the language we employ in our communications. We must ensure that our words reflect the ethical people we ought to be. Once discussions move toward the use of foul language, we can choose to raise a respectable objection or step aside. We also know that foul or offensive language corrupts good manners. Foul language attacks the very core of our ethics and morals by chipping away at them. Before long, that strong and unacceptable language becomes the norm for those who were hitherto very clean. This is a very important boundary because it is out of the abundance of the heart that the mouth speaks. If what the mouth speaks is effectively junk, one can only imagine what the heart is filled with. This is where our ethics as individuals arise from; we must guard our words and also our hearts with all diligence. It is a bit like hear no evil, speak no evil.

Composure on the other hand is about being in control, especially during arguments or presentations. Simple advice would be to note down on paper the points we would like to challenge. This helps us avoid speaking over others, and it also gives a semblance of professionalism.

Besides, as part of composure, we must recognize that it is not about us as people and likely not about the individuals with whom we are conversing. There is a greater purpose or objective, and there is a greater person who must take preeminence in all cases. God and what He thinks about what is happening is of the greatest importance at all times.

Take the example of Job—and every other person who feels hard done by. As long as he makes the discourse about himself, the discussion will lead toward depression or prideful anger. However, if we make the discussion and focus about God and God's purpose, we recognize our frailties and inadequacies and learn to lean on God's abilities.

It is not about winning or losing the argument; it is about the truth. We must remember that facts are good, but they change. Only the truth remains constant and unchanging regardless of perspective.

Finally, however much society has pressured us into thinking it is about me, myself, and I, we must disabuse our minds and refocus the basis of all thoughts, words, and actions on God. This will help keep our language clean and our words devoid of exaggerations and white lies.

Act First and Ask for Forgiveness Later

On this basis, they feel justified to subvert laid-down rules and procedures with the mind-set that they can always ask for forgiveness. To them, it is easier to ask for forgiveness than address proper procedures. Instead, they must refuse the urge to embark on an unapproved and potentially wrong action.

The implication of this is grave. How would we feel if someone offended us repeatedly and each time asks for forgiveness—but goes right back to offending? After a while, the asking for forgiveness is no longer heartfelt. When it becomes mechanical, the offender's heart is not grieved, and they are no longer remorseful. Asking for forgiveness becomes a "check-the-box" exercise. It is highly unlikely that such "apologies" will get any forgiveness because they are not coming from the heart.

When we are effectively choosing to do wrong, it could also be that we are doing the right thing wrongly or following the wrong process to do the "right thing." Regardless, it is a choice we are making. We should always choose to do right and follow ethical processes to do the same and not rely on the uncertainty of forgiveness.

Many of us actually want to cover up deliberate wrongdoing with a good act or a good story instead of simply apologizing and receiving due forgiveness. This says a lot about our ethical standards as individuals, and we need to do the right thing. If we are in such a position and can respectably challenge or ask questions about the instructions for clarity, then we should. However, we should not:

- make a habit of deliberately doing the wrong thing and then trying to apologize later.

- cover up wrongdoing by trying to use nice words to paint disobedience in nice colors.

- try to cover up wrongdoing by submerging or mixing the same in other unrelated good acts.

We must raise the bar of our ethical behaviors beyond all of these instances.

Applying Different Standards for Different People or Scenarios

Even though everybody's situations are different, everyone deserves to be treated fairly and with respect regardless of the baggage they carry. However, we must be careful with how we show favoritism to people. We should not deliberately cause one to be disadvantaged over another for any reason.

With a heavenly perspective, we must recognize that every soul matter to God counts. Within every human organization, we will have cliques. People will always flock to those with whom they have similar likes and dislikes; it is simply an expression of human freedom of association. I have no issues with that, but we must try not to unduly practice exclusion or treat others negatively.

The stranger today may become the best friend of tomorrow. We must maximize every interaction with everyone. We must abide by a minimum level of personal ethical behavior that must apply to all; it is a characteristic of who we are and not of those we relate with.

Eye Service—but Not Full Service

This stems from a desire to please the leader—not necessarily to do the right thing—and that is where we get it wrong. In itself, we must respect the leader, share in the leader's vision, and do all we can to ensure its realization. However, that is not the same as competing for the leader's affection by outdoing one another to show who can best please them based on our perspectives of their needs.

Eye service leads to unhealthy competition between those that should be cooperating to achieve the leader's goals or the organization's goals. It depletes available resources that could have been channeled in better ways. Those who partake in this behavior often require some form of affirmation or positional recognition from the leader, and when such is not forthcoming, it leads to being disgruntled or even backbiting. From an ethics point of view, we need to check our tendency to display eye service and focus on adding lasting value in line with organizational objectives.

Subtle Deceit by Seeking to Impress

This occurs when we try to project an exaggerated—often false—image of ourselves to others to win their affection or affirmation. Surely, we should all strive to become better versions of ourselves, and for that, we need to work on daily improving ourselves in every area where we desire improvement, but it is a different thing to project who we are not to someone else to achieve our goals. After a while, the true self shows—and the relationship turns sour.

When a person of high standards begins to emulate the world to get affirmation—or a job, a contract, or a spouse—they will find that even when they succeed in that endeavor, keeping such a trophy will require the charade to be kept up for much longer. Otherwise, they are right back to zero points—and they may even be referred to as a hypocrite. We need to be ourselves, our authentic selves.

Chapter 9

Ethics, Excuses, and Misconceptions

The very foundation of ethics is threatened once we feel we are justified during difficult times to put aside the same ethics that are meant to regulate and guide our behavior and to a large extent help pull us out of difficult situations. Many people cite extenuating circumstances as a sufficient reason to put aside all rules and deploy "whatever works" regardless of the negative implant of such. This argument presupposes that observing ethical standards would be insufficient to lift us out of such situations and confines ethical standards to "good times." However, excusing ourselves from observing proper ethical standards only leads to effectively unacceptable circumstances, failing in the aspect of the process adopted in achieving the end desired.

There are several excuses we give:

1. We tend to use our disabilities to excuse ourselves from keeping to high ethical standards: "I stole because I didn't have food to eat." While this sounds plausible, we have to also consider those who refused to steal and rather sought assistance from others to help alleviate their situations. They also did not have food, but they chose to retain their integrity by choosing a solution that helped them retain their integrity.

2. "Since I do not want to be alienated, I choose to lower my standards." The impact and pressure of wanting to "belong" have made many lower their ethical standards. The adage that states "One with God is a majority" is possibly no longer fashionable in a world seeking the affirmation of unknown persons on social media. Consider the many youths who succumb to trying drugs and promiscuity simply because their "friends" pressured them to do it. Some end up losing their lives, their dignity, and the friends who pressured them into the unethical acts. Lowering our standards always leaves a bitter taste, and the enduring sham will not be easily wiped away.

3. "I meant well, but I had to go against my ethics to achieve the bigger objective." This is different from working together to achieve a laudable objective. It's about bending the truth and doing whatever it takes to land that big account and get a fat bonus as a result. Some people falsify data by making it look good to sell a story that will land them a successful presentation. In today's world, it comes in many names, including *spin, whitewash,* and *massaging the truth.* This leads to painting something that we know is bad in glowing colors or downplaying how bad they are to the extent of making them acceptable to the public. People who do this want to justify their actions by stating that this is how they see it—and "there are several views of the same issue." However, the truth has no shades. It is unchanging and is not subject to varying interpretations.

4. There are examples in the Bible. "If Moses married a non-Israelite as a man of God and was not punished by God, I can do the same." Many of us quote prominent figure or cite examples of their actions to justify our unethical actions. However, standards are not tied to individuals. They are the standards all individuals should live by. So simply

because prominent figures—including political leaders, celebrities, and thought leaders—say or do something that is wrong, it does not give us the license to lower our own ethical standards.

Chapter 10

The Impact of Diminished Ethical Behavior

Diminished ethical behavior can be detrimental and dangerous to individuals, families, and societies.

Individuals

The symptoms of underlying ethical problems are evident everywhere in the twenty-first century. Many of these symptoms are due to a foundation of broken ethical rules that must be addressed in order for the issues to disappear. Many people are rude, selfish, indulgent, and permissive. They do not care about the impact their words have when spoken openly to others. In addition, their promises are broken easily. Words are now cheap, and they are no longer regarded as bonds. The level of commitment to relationships is at an all-time low when compared to previous generations. Today's generation lacks interest and skill in long-term commitment. Values are also at an all-time low. So many lies and innuendos are told today, especially on social media, that it is clear that many people lack empathy and care for others.

Families

Many families have been eroded today because of poor ethical values. Many people enter marriages without the principles of true commitment, faithfulness, and loyalty. Many people find it difficult to commit through both the good and bad times. Divorce is rising at an alarming rate. One in two Christian marriages ends in divorce! This can be explained through the many character defects that prevent people from being tolerant and patient with their spouses. Marriage has been turned into a mere reproduction center for children. Parents have shown a smaller investment of time, love, and resources in training their children. That lack of discipline goes unchecked, resulting in children growing up with many negative emotions, including rage, anger, and hatred. Bullying, racism, harassment, substance abuse, and delinquency are also increasing.

Society/Nation

Families are the basic unit of society. If the families are rotten, then society will also be rotten. Many societies have become cities without walls. There are no rules—just chaos everywhere. The foundation of our current world is shaken. This is a world where:

- It is advised to always look for your own interests. There is no free lunch.

- Rules are promoted over relationships.

- Lies are preferred to the truth.

- Marriage is been redefined daily.

- Busyness and shady business are promoted in many nations.

- Abortion is legalized.

- Marijuana is legalized.

There is a lack of order, justice, and love in our current world. Leaders of many nations lack the decorum, integrity, and character needed to lead. Many individuals are simply pursuing their interests and ambitions.

The handling of the current COVID-19 pandemic in many nations has exposed the impact of diminished ethical behaviors. Some decisions have been made by certain leaders in order to score political points instead of prioritizing the safety and well-being of their citizens. In some nations, there is no respect for the rules or laws that have been put in place, and some governmental restrictions are not even obeyed by religious leaders and institutions. Some celebrities have let down their guard by ignoring the lockdown protocols and stay-at-home orders that have been issued by their governments. There is great neglect for ethical behaviors!

The dangers of diminished ethical behaviors are grievous, and there is no way to escape from these individual, family, and societal problems. The solutions will be in teaching, promoting, encouraging, and modeling sound ethical behaviors. The roots of diminished ethical behavior must be dealt with on individual, family, and societal levels:

> How shall we escape if we ignore so great a salvation? (Hebrews 2:3 NIV).

Epilogue

Real-Life Ethical Issues

These are real-life examples. The goal is for the readers to learn from them. These can be discussed in a group setting in a nonjudgmental manner. Even though the readers need to take into consideration the settings, environments, and religious and cultural background of the individual examples, the overall objective of upholding the highest ethical and moral standards cuts across all cultures, races, religions, and nations:

1. At a wedding ceremony, the bride delayed her arrival for more than fifty minutes. The emcee suggested starting to worship to pass the time until the bride arrived.

2. A guest minister was invited to minister from out of country for a weekend program, and he insisted

on staying for few more days after the conference to rest and visit different areas of interest.

3. A visiting senior pastor brought some gifts to honor all pastors attending the conference where he would be ministering. One of the protocol girls loved the gifts and picked one for herself, but she approached the senior pastor to make a demand for it.

4. If you are blessed with the ministration of a guest speaker during a weekend conference, how will you respond?

5. A member of a church approached a guest pastor preaching in their church to come inspect and bless his new property without telling his pastor.

6. A man and a woman came to welcome my wife and I at Heathrow Airport. They collected our luggage trolleys and wheeled them to their car. Upon reaching the car, the guy lifted all the luggage in my trolley and left the second trolley. I ended up lifting the luggage with the help of my wife. When asked why he did that, he replied, "The lady can lift the luggage on the trolley she wheeled for us."

7. A young adult approached her senior pastor's wife to wish her a happy birthday. She said, "So, you are an Aries." The senior pastor's wife was speechless.

8. An elderly man was attending a conference. While struggling with his personal belongings in the reception area of the hotel, many young adults greeted him warmly and passed him by.

9. A family handed a Christmas gift to their friend. The friend discovered the gift had once been given to the friend.

10. A guest speaker visiting a church was interested in knowing more about the host church and the city. He asked some of the workers and leaders about the demographics of the church and the city, but they had no clue.

11. A protocol member who helped a guest speaker to his room on last day of the conference went to the bedroom of the guest speaker to drop off his bag, and the protocol member discovered he had forgotten his wallet in the guest speaker's room.

12. An associate minister stopped returning his tithe to his home church because he felt the church was spending too much money on conferences, especially on publicity and honorarium for guest speakers.

13. A worker at one of our parishes bought a new car. He brought the car to church and parked it behind the guest speaker's car so the anointed guest speaker would be the one to dedicate it.

14. A leader in a growing church saw no reason for notifying his pastor when he would not be showing up for certain church programs.

15. The senior pastor of a growing Pentecostal church noticed that one of his active workers (GS) had been away from church without his knowledge for a few weeks. The pastor sent a text message to GS and his close friend. GS's friend replied, "He is fine, sir. He is the best person to explain why he has not been in church." When the pastor eventually met with GS, he said he had told his immediate leader (departmental head) that he wanted to take some time off.

16. In a busy emergency room, a nurse saw nothing wrong about not saying hello to her colleagues when reporting for duty.

17. A long-serving active employee of an organization handed over her letter of resignation with one week's notice. She still expected her entire compensation.

18. Some employees of an organization walked away from their jobs because they felt the discipline meted out by the executive team to one of their colleagues was too much for his errors.

19. A volunteer decided to reduce her time in a nongovernmental organization (NGO) without informing the executive team of the NGO.

20. An active man in a church believed a woman could not successfully lead a church.

21. A nonbelieving physician insisted that one of his from students stop posting his daily living nugget on their old student platform because he it was religious and self-promoting. However, the physician kept posting myriad political messages

and videos and sharing his ideological views on the platform.

22. A pastor said, "I don't care what I wear to the pulpit when I am preaching." He felt it was traditional and outdated to insist on pastors wearing a suit to preach.

23. A single lady saw nothing wrong about spending a weekend in the same room with her fiancé while planning for their wedding.

24. During the COVID-19 pandemic lockdown, a pastor said, "The government cannot shut down any church." He refused to shut down his church building for worshippers.

25. A pastor was fond of removing cash from the church collection before counting/account reconciliation every Sunday in order to buy gas and food for his church staff as a way of rewarding their services.

26. A Christian man believed a Christian who knows how to pray could never suffer from depression or any other mental health crises.

27. A woman said, "The black race is a cursed race from the descendants of Canaan, and there is no way they can compete or match the white race."

28. A family was refusing to vaccinate their children because they believed vaccines contained chemicals, including mercury, that can harm children or cause autism.

29. A family with ten children would not use contraception because they believed the government was using it to control a particular race or religion.

30. A pastor told his congregation not to use medications for any ailments and to believe in the power of prayer.

Manufactured by Amazon.ca
Bolton, ON

30966315R00065